Wind

by Grace Hansen

Abdo
WEATHER
Kids

abdopublishing.com

Published by Abdo Kids, a division of ABDO, PO Box 398166, Minneapolis, Minnesota 55439.

Copyright © 2016 by Abdo Consulting Group, Inc. International copyrights reserved in all countries. No part of this book may be reproduced in any form without written permission from the publisher.

Printed in the United States of America, North Mankato, Minnesota.

052015

092015

 THIS BOOK CONTAINS RECYCLED MATERIALS

Photo Credits: iStock, NASA, Shutterstock

Production Contributors: Teddy Borth, Jennie Forsberg, Grace Hansen

Design Contributors: Laura Rask, Dorothy Toth

Library of Congress Control Number: 2014958421

Cataloging-in-Publication Data

Hansen, Grace.

 Wind / Grace Hansen.

  p. cm. -- (Weather)

ISBN 978-1-62970-936-9

Includes index.

1. Winds--Juvenile literature.   I. Title.

551.51--dc23

              2014958421

Table of Contents

What is Wind?

You can feel wind. You can hear wind. You can see trees blow in the wind.

4

5

Wind is moving air. You cannot see wind. But it is powerful.

Wind can be a light breeze.

Or it can be a strong gust.

Wind can move in any direction.

9

Air is always pushing down on Earth. This is called **atmospheric pressure**. There are high-pressure areas. And there are low-pressure areas.

11

Hot air is lighter than cold air. Light air creates low-pressure areas.

Cold air is heavier. Heavy air creates high-pressure areas.

15

High-pressure areas move to low-pressure areas. This evens everything out. We feel this movement. It is wind!

Wind Direction

Wind comes from the north and south. The Earth spins. The spin changes the wind's direction. This is why wind can come from anywhere.

19

Amazing Wind!

Wind moves weather. It carries heat and **moisture**. Wind also moves seeds and rocks. Wind is also used for **energy**.

20

How Wind Forms

Cool Air

Cool air sinks

 **high pressure**

Wind

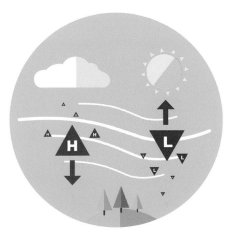

Warm Air

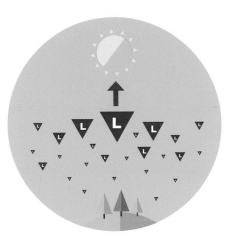

Warm air rises

low pressure

Air moves from a **high pressure**
area to a **low pressure** area.
We feel this movement of air as **wind**.

22

Glossary

atmospheric pressure – pressure from the weight of air pushing down on Earth. Air pressure tells us what kind of weather to expect.

energy – usable power that comes from wind.

moisture – a small amount of water that makes something wet.

Index

abdokids.com

Use this code to log on to abdokids.com and access crafts, games, videos, and more!

Abdo Kids Code:
WWK9369